Wishing to hearten a timid lamp

great night lights all her stars.

为鼓舞一盏羞怯的寒灯

长夜点亮了满天的繁星

流 萤 集

· 英汉对照 ·

[印]泰戈尔 著　王钦刚 译

（根据THE MACMILLAN COMPANY 1928年版译）

FIREFLIES

图书在版编目(CIP)数据

流萤集:英汉对照/(印)泰戈尔著;王钦刚译.—成都:四川文艺出版社,2019.5
ISBN 978-7-5411-5415-7

Ⅰ.①流… Ⅱ.①泰…②王… Ⅲ.①英语—汉语—对照读物②诗集—印度—现代 Ⅳ.①H319.4:I

中国版本图书馆CIP数据核字(2019)第074865号

LIU YING JI
流萤集

[印] 泰戈尔 著
王钦刚 译

责任编辑　燕啸波
封面设计　叶　茂
内文设计　史小燕
责任校对　段　敏
责任印制　唐　茵

出版发行	四川文艺出版社(成都市槐树街2号)
网　　址	www.scwys.com
电　　话	028-86259287(发行部)　028-86259303(编辑部)
传　　真	028-86259306
邮购地址	成都市槐树街2号四川文艺出版社邮购部　610031
排　　版	四川最近文化传播有限公司
印　　刷	成都东江印务有限公司
成品尺寸	130mm×185mm　开　本　32开
印　　张	5　字　数　100千
版　　次	2019年5月第一版　印　次　2019年5月第一次印刷
书　　号	ISBN 978-7-5411-5415-7
定　　价	32.00元

版权所有·侵权必究。如有质量问题,请与出版社联系更换。028-86259301

FIREFLIES had their origin in China and Japan where thoughts were very often claimed from me in my handwriting on fans and pieces of silk.

——Tagore

《流萤集》
源于我的中国和日本之行
彼时我常常应人之请
将我的点滴思想
题写于扇子和丝绢上

——泰戈尔

1

My fancies are fireflies, —
Specks of living light
twinkling in the dark.

我的梦是流萤
点点飞光
在黑暗中闪烁着光明

2

The voice of wayside pansies,
that do not attract the careless glance,
murmurs in these desultory lines.

幽径旁的三色堇
并不吸引漫不经心的眼神
而在这零乱的诗行里低吟

3

In the drowsy dark caves of the mind
dreams build their nest with fragments
dropped from day's caravan.

心灵的洞穴中困倦幽暗
睡梦用白昼遗落的碎片
在那里筑起自己的家园

4

Spring scatters the petals of flowers

that are not for the fruits of the future,

but for the moment's whim.

花瓣并不为明天的硕果着想

而只为一时的兴致绽放

于是在春天里飘零四方

5

Joy freed from the bond of earth's slumber

rushes into numberless leaves

and dances in the air for a day.

欢乐挣脱大地沉睡的束缚

冲入无尽的叶丛

在空中终日欢舞

6

My words that are slight

may lightly dance upon time's waves

when my works heavy with import have

gone down.

当我语重心长的著作已悄无声响

而我轻盈的言语

或许还翩翩起舞在岁月的波光上

7

Mind's underground moths

grow filmy wings

and take a farewell flight

in the sunset sky.

心底隐秘的飞蛾

生出了纤薄的翅膀

在黄昏的天空中

做一次告别的飞翔

8

The butterfly counts not months but moments,

and has time enough.

蝴蝶不计岁月

而以瞬间丈量

时光因此而悠长

9

My thoughts, like sparks, ride on winged surprises,
carrying a single laughter.

我那如火花般的思想
载了一程欢笑
乘着插翅的惊喜飞翔

10

The tree gazes in love at its own beautiful shadow
which yet it never can grasp.

树木深情凝视自己的倩影
却永远不能把它抓在手中

11

Let my love, like sunlight, surround you

and yet give you illumined freedom.

让我的爱像阳光围绕你左右

而又给你熠熠生辉的自由

12

Days are coloured bubbles

that float upon the surface of fathomless night.

白昼是五彩缤纷的泡影

在深邃的黑夜表面浮动

13

My offerings are too timid to claim your remembrance,
and therefore you may remember them.

我的奉献羞怯得不敢奢求你的铭记
由此你或许会将它们记在心底

14

Leave out my name from the gift
if it be a burden,
but keep my song.

如果我的名字成为负担
请把它从献礼中遗忘
只留下我的诗篇

15

April, like a child,

writes hieroglyphs on dust with flowers,

wipes them away and forgets.

四月，像个孩子

用花朵在尘土上写下象形文字

然后擦去，并忘记

16

Memory, the priestess,

kills the present,

and offers its heart to the shrine of the dead past.

回忆，这女祭司

杀死了现时

并把它的心献给逝去往昔的神祠

17

From the solemn gloom of the temple,
children run out to sit in the dust.
God watches them play
and forgets the priest.

逃离神庙肃穆的幽谧
孩子们坐在尘土里
神明注视着他们嬉戏
于是忘记了那祭司

18

My mind starts up at some flash

on the flow of its thoughts

like a brook at a sudden liquid note of its own

that is never repeated.

我的心在思绪的灵光乍现中醒来

正如小溪

在迸发的从不往复的流音里

春暖花开

19

In the mountain, stillness surges up

to explore its own height;

in the lake, movement stands still

to contemplate its own depth.

山峦寂静

汹涌中以探其高峻

湖泊汹涌

寂静中以思其幽深

20

The departing night's one kiss
on the closed eyes of morning
glows in the star of dawn.

即将离去的黑夜
吻在黎明紧闭的双眸上
羞红了晨星的脸庞

21

Maiden, thy beauty is like a fruit
which is yet to mature,
tense with an unyielding secret.

少女呵,你的美恰似
一枚尚未成熟的果实
焦虑里藏着一个倔强的秘密

22

Sorrow that has lost its memory

is like the dumb dark hours

that have no bird songs

but only the cricket's chirp.

失去了记忆的悲伤

如暗哑的黑暗时光

那里没有鸟的鸣唱

而只有幽幽的蛩响

23

Bigotry tries to keep truth safe in its hand
with a grip that kills it.

偏执想保护真理于手中
真理却因被紧握而丧生

24

Wishing to hearten a timid lamp
great night lights all her stars.

为鼓舞一盏羞怯的寒灯
长夜点亮了满天的繁星

25

Though he holds in his arms the earth-bride,
the sky is ever immensely away.

天空将大地新娘拥在怀里
他却永远与她无限仳离

26

God seeks comrades and claims love,
the Devil seeks slaves and claims obedience.

神明求同道而索爱
恶魔寻奴仆而求从

27

The soil in return for her service

keeps the tree tied to her,

the sky asks nothing and leaves it free.

作为养育的报偿

泥土把树木束缚身旁

天空则一无所求

任树木自由生长

28

Jewel-like the immortal

does not boast of its length of years

but of the scintillating point of its moment.

不朽者如同宝石一样

并不自诩其岁月之长

而自豪于瞬间的闪亮

29

The child ever dwells in the mystery
of ageless time,
unobscured by the dust of history.

孩童永居于不朽时光的神秘
历史的尘埃也无法将其蒙蔽

30

A light laughter in the steps of creation
carries it swiftly across time.

在创世的筚路山林
一丝浅笑
便携着它轻盈地穿越光阴

31

One who was distant came near to me in the morning,
and still nearer when taken away by night.

斯人相距遥远
清晨走近身边
夜晚离去
驻我心间

32

White and pink oleanders meet
and make merry in different dialects.

白的和粉的夹竹桃相见
用不同的方言谈笑甚欢

33

When peace is active sweeping its dirt,
it is storm.

当平静奋力拂去灰尘
风暴便降临

34

The lake lies low by the hill,
a tearful entreaty of love
at the foot of the inflexible.

湖泊盈盈泪眼
拜倒在山前
奈何他心意如磐

35

There smiles the Divine Child
among his playthings of unmeaning clouds
and ephemeral lights and shadows.

在索然无味的云朵
和转瞬即逝的光影之间把玩
神的孩子露出笑颜

36

The breeze whispers to the lotus,

"What is thy secret?"

"It is myself," says the lotus,

"Steal it and I disappear!"

微风对莲花低语

"什么是你的秘密?"

"是我自己",莲花说,

"偷去这秘密,我便会消失。"

37

The freedom of the storm and the bondage of the stem
join hands in the dance of swaying branches.

风暴的自由和树干的束缚
携手于枝条的摇曳的轻舞

38

The jasmine's lisping of love to the sun
is her flowers.

茉莉的花瓣
便是她对太阳爱恋的呢喃

39

The tyrant claims freedom to kill freedom
and yet to keep it for himself.

暴君要求扼杀自由的自由
但只许他自己拥有

40

Gods, tired of their paradise, envy man.

诸神厌倦了他们的乐园
开始羡慕人间

41

Clouds are hills in vapour,
hills are clouds in stone,—
a phantasy in time's dream.

云是气蒸霞蔚之山
山是乱石穿空之云
这便是时光的如梦似幻

42

While God waits for His temple to be built of love,
men brings stones.

上帝期待他的庙宇用爱建造
人类却带来了石料

43

I touch God in my song
as the hill touches the far-away sea
with its waterfall.

我以我的歌通向上苍
正如山以瀑布通向遥远的海洋

44

Light finds her treasure of colours
through the antagonism of clouds.

通过云的反光
阳光发现了她色彩的宝藏

45

My heart to-day smiles at its past night of tears
like a wet tree glistening in the sun
after the rain is over.

今天，我的心
笑对昨夜的泪水
正如雨后淋湿的树
在阳光下熠熠生辉

46

I have thanked the trees that have made my life fruitful,
but have failed to remember the grass that has ever kept it green.

我感谢过树林
曾使我的人生硕果累累
却忘记了小草
曾使我的人生碧草如茵

47

The one without second is emptiness,
the other one makes it true.

独一无二是空
无独有偶成真

48

Life's errors cry for the merciful beauty
that can modulate their isolation
into a harmony with the whole.

生命中的错误
乞求仁慈之美
将它们的孤立无助
融入整体的和睦

49

They expect thanks for the banished nest
because their cage is shapely and secure.

因为它们的笼子美观而牢靠
它们期待感激被放弃的旧巢

50

In love I pay my endless debt to thee
for what thou art.

无论您是怎样的人
我用无尽的爱偿还您

51

The pond sends up its lyrics from its dark
in lilies,
and the sun says, they are good.

百合,小池的抒情诗
在其幽暗处亭亭玉立
她们赢得了太阳的赞许

52

Your calumny against the great is impious,

it hurts yourself;

against the small it is mean,

for it hurts the victim.

诽谤伟大者乃不敬

伤及自己

中伤渺小者乃卑鄙

殃及无辜

53

The first flower that blossomed on this earth

was an invitation to the unborn song.

大地上最先盛开的花朵

是向未来之歌的邀约

54

Dawn—the many-coloured flower—fades,
and then the simple light-fruit,
the sun appears.

黎明
这色彩斑斓之花刚凋零
太阳
这光华纯粹之果便登场

55

The muscle that has a doubt of its wisdom
throttles the voice that would cry.

肌肉对自身的智慧没有信心
便扼杀要呼喊的声音

56

The wind tries to take the flame by storm

only to blow it out.

风试图抢夺火焰

却只能将其吹散

57

Life's play is swift,

Life's playthings fall behind one by one

and are forgotten.

人生的游戏转瞬即逝

人生的玩具一一抛弃

并被忘记

58

My flower, seek not thy paradise

in a fool's buttonhole.

我的花儿呵
不要在愚人的扣眼
寻觅你的乐园

59

Thou hast risen late, my crescent moon,

but my night bird is still awake to greet thee.

我的新月呵
你姗姗来迟
而我的夜莺依然不寐
等候着向你致意

60

Darkness is the veiled bride
silently waiting for the errant light
to return to her bosom.

黑暗是蒙着面纱的新娘
静静地等待着出轨的光
重回她的身旁

61

Trees are the earth's endless effort to
speak to the listening heaven.

树木是大地无尽的付出
向聆听的天宇倾诉

62

The burden of self is lightened
when I laugh at myself.

当我自嘲
负担渐消

63

The weak can be terrible
because they try furiously to appear strong.

以弱示强
雨暴风狂

64

The wind of heaven blows,
The anchor desperately clutches the mud,
and my boat is beating its breast against
the chain.

天堂的风吹起
锚绝望地抓紧淤泥
而我的小船
用胸膛撞击着锁链

65

The spirit of death is one,

the spirit of life is many.

When God is dead, religion becomes one.

死之魂是一

生之魂是多

当神死去

宗教合一

66

The blue of the sky longs for the earth's green,
the wind between them sighs, "Alas".

天之蓝渴望地之绿
徒留其间风的叹息

67

Day's pain muffled by its own glare,
burns among stars in the night.

白昼的苦痛掩盖于自身的光芒
便在夜晚的繁星间闪亮

68

The stars crowd round the virgin night
in silent awe at her loneliness
that can never be touched.

群星簇拥着处子般的夜
对着她永远无法触及的孤寂
默默地敬而畏之

69

The cloud gives all its gold
to the departing sun
and greets the rising moon
with only a pale smile.

云彩把所有的金黄
都给了离去的夕阳
只一抹淡淡的微笑
来致意初升的月亮

70

He who does good comes to the temple gate,
he who loves reaches the shrine.

善者止于门廊
爱者抵达庙堂

71

Flower, have pity for the worm,

it is not a bee,

its love is a blunder and a burden.

花呵

可怜这小虫吧

它并不是蜜蜂

它的爱是疏忽与负重

72

With the ruins of terror's triumph

children build their doll's house.

用恐怖的胜利之残垣断壁

孩子建起他们玩偶的居室

73

The lamp waits through the long day of neglect
for the flame's kiss in the night.

在白昼的煎熬里无人问津
灯盏期待夜间火焰的亲吻

74

Feathers in the dust lying lazily content
have forgotten their sky.

慵懒惬意地躺在尘埃中
羽毛忘记了它们的天空

75

The flower which is single
need not envy the thorns
that are numerous.

孤零的花枝
无须羡慕
丛生的荆棘

76

The world suffers most from the disinterested tyranny
of its well-wisher.

世上最大的苦痛
来自好心人无私的专政

77

We gain freedom when we have paid the full price
for our right to live.

我们为生存权利
付出全部代价之日
便是我们赢得自由之时

78

Your careless gifts of a moment,
like the meteors of an autumn night,
catch fire in the depth of my being.

你那一刻无心的馈赠
宛如秋夜的流星
在我生命深处燃起烈火熊熊

79

The faith waiting in the heart of a seed

promises a miracle of life

which cannot prove at once.

信念，等候在种子的心中

许下一个生命的奇迹

虽然无法立刻来验证

80

Spring hesitates at winter's door,

but the mango blossom rashly runs out to him

before her time and meets her doom.

春还在冬的门口徘徊

为时尚早

杧果花却迫不及待

终至厄运到来

81

The world is the ever-changing foam
that floats on the surface of a sea of silence.

世界是变幻无穷的泡影
在寂静之海的表面浮动

82

The two separated shores mingle their voices
in a song of unfathomed tears.

分离的两岸将声音汇合
共唱一曲无尽的泪之歌

83

As a river in the sea,
work finds its fulfilment
in the depth of leisure.

如同江河入海
劳动在闲暇的深处
觅得满足

84

I lingered on my way till thy cherry tree lost its blossom,
but the azalea brings to me, my love, thy forgiveness.

我在路上徘徊
直至你的樱桃树花儿开败
我的爱人呵
杜鹃花却把你的宽恕带来

85

Thy shy little pomegranate bud,
blushing to-day behind her veil,
will burst into a passionate flower
tomorrow when I am away.

你那羞怯的小石榴花蕾
今天在她面纱后羞红了脸庞
明天当我远走他方
她将会热烈绽放

86

The clumsiness of power spoils the key,
and uses the pickaxe.

笨拙的权力弄坏了钥匙
便把镐头举起

87

Birth is from the mystery of night
into the greater mystery of day.

生是从夜之神秘
进入昼之更神秘

88

These paper boats of mine are meant to dance on the ripples of hours,
and not to reach any destination.

我的这些纸船
愿在流光的涟漪上翩跹
而不想停靠任何港湾

89

Migratory songs wing from my heart
and seek their nests in your voice of love.

流浪的歌声飞出我的心田
在你爱的呼唤里寻觅家园

90

The sea of danger, doubt and denial
around man's little island of certainty
challenges him to dare the unknown.

危险、怀疑与否定的海湾
将凡人的永恒小岛环绕
激励着他直面未知的挑战

91

Love punishes when it forgives,

and injured beauty by its awful silence.

爱的宽恕也是鞭挞

残缺之美以可怕的沉默来惩罚

92

You live alone and unrecompensed

because they are afraid of your great worth.

你壮志未酬而遗世独立

因世人畏你之绝世价值

93

The same sun is newly born in new lands
in a ring of endless dawns.

无尽的黎明
旧日得新生

94

God's world is ever renewed by death,
a Titan's ever crushed by its own existence.

上帝的世界由死亡不断更新
巨人的世界总是碾压于自身

95

The glow-worm while exploring the dust
never knows that the stars are in the sky.

在尘土里探寻的萤火虫
从不知晓繁星居于天空

96

The tree is of to-day, the flower is old,
it brings with it the message
of the immemorial seed.

树在今日
花自往昔
它携来远古种子的讯息

97

Each rose that comes brings me greetings

from the Rose of an eternal spring.

每一朵玫瑰盛开

都把永恒之春里玫瑰的问候带来

98

God honours me when I work,

He loves me when I sing.

我劳作,上帝敬我

我欢歌,上帝爱我

99

My love of to-day finds no home
in the nest deserted by yesterday's love.

在昨日之爱抛弃的旧巢内
我今日之爱无家可归

100

The fire of pain traces for my soul
a luminous path across her sorrow.

痛苦的火焰为我的魂灵
照亮穿越悲伤的光明小径

101

The grass survives the hill

through its resurrections from countless deaths.

无数次死而复生

小草比大山长青

102

Thou hast vanished from my reach

leaving an impalpable touch in the blue of

the sky,

an invisible image in the wind moving

among the shadows.

你突然消失在我眼前

留下无形的一抹在天空的蔚蓝

以及风中的幻象,摇曳在暗影间

103

In pity for the desolate branch
spring leaves to it a kiss that fluttered in a
lonely leaf.

春天对萧疏的枝条心生恻隐
便给它留下
曾在孤叶上翩跹飞舞的一吻

104

The shy shadow in the garden

loves the sun in silence,

Flowers guess the secret, and smile,

while the leaves whisper.

园中羞怯的影子

默默爱恋着红日

花儿笑着，猜中了秘密

而叶子在窃窃私语

105

I leave no trace of wings in the air,

but I am glad I have had my flight.

天空没有留下翅膀的痕迹

但我为曾经的飞翔而欣喜

106

The fireflies, twinkling among leaves,
make the stars wonder.

流萤闪烁在叶间
令繁星为之惊叹

107

The mountain remains unmoved
at its seeming defeat by the mist.

面对雾霭表面上的获胜
山岳依旧岿然不动

108

While the rose said to the sun
"I shall ever remember thee."
her petals fell to the dust.

当玫瑰对太阳说
"我将永远记住你"
她的花瓣便零落成泥

109

Hills are the earth's gesture of despair
for the unreachable.

山峦是大地
向遥不可及之处
摆出的绝望姿势

110

Though the thorn in thy flower pricked me,

O Beauty,

I am grateful.

尽管你花间的刺

给我痛的记忆

美人呵

我依然心怀感激

111

The world knows that the few

are more than the many.

世人懂得

少胜于多

112

Let not my love be a burden on you,

my friend,

know that it pays itself.

朋友
别让我的爱给你重压
要知道它自有报答

113

Dawn plays her lute before the gate of darkness,

and is content to vanish when the sun

comes out.

黎明在暗夜的门前弹琴
当旭日东升便甘心隐身

114

Beauty is truth's smile

when she beholds her own face

in a perfect mirror.

美在无瑕的镜中
看见自己的面孔
美便是真的笑容

115

The dew-drop knows the sun

only within its own tiny orb.

露珠以为太阳
只在它微小的泪滴里闪光

116

Forlorn thoughts from the forsaken hives of
all ages,
swarming in the air, hum round my heart
and seek my voice.

孤寂的思想
逃出万世遗弃的蜂房
云集在空中
萦绕我的心头哼唱
来寻觅我的声响

117

The desert is imprisoned in the wall
of its unbounded barrenness.

荒漠囚禁于自己
无边贫瘠的高墙里

118

In the thrill of little leaves

I see the air's invisible dance,

and in their glimmering

the secret heart-beats of the sky.

在细叶的轻轻震颤中

我看见空气隐形的舞蹈

在它们的闪闪微光中

我看见天空隐秘的心跳

119

You are like a flowering tree,

amazed when I praise you for your gifts.

你像一棵树,繁花盛开

当我赞美你的天才

你喜出望外

120

The earth's sacrificial fire

flames up in her trees

scattering sparks in flowers.

大地的祭火

在林间爆发

火星飞溅成花

121

Forests, the clouds of earth,

hold up to the sky their silence,

and clouds from above come down

in resonant showers.

森林是大地之云

以沉默向天空延伸

而天空之云

则报以落雨纷纷

122

The world speaks to me in pictures,

my soul answers in music.

世界以图画与我说话

我的心便以音乐作答

123

The sky tells its beads all night

on the countless stars

in memory of the sun.

为把太阳纪念

天空整夜细数

无尽星辰的珠串

124

The darkness of night, like pain, is dumb,

the darkness of dawn, like peace, is silent.

黑夜之暗,如苦痛,喑哑无声

黎明之暗,如和平,缄默无言

125

Pride engraves his frowns in stones,

love offers her surrender in flowers.

傲慢颦眉于石

爱情倾倒以花

126

The obsequious brush curtails truth

in deference to the canvas which is narrow.

谄媚的画笔偷梁换柱

以迎合狭窄的画布

127

The hill in its longing for the far-away sky
wishes to be like the cloud
with its endless urge of seeking.

山丘憧憬着遥远的天空
希望像云一样
充满追寻的无限激情

128

To justify their own spilling of ink
they spell the day as night.

为给自己溢洒的墨水辩解
他们把白天写作黑夜

129

Profit smiles on goodness

when the good is profitable.

当善带来利好

利便对善微笑

130

In its swelling pride

the bubble doubts the truth of the sea,

and laughs and bursts into emptiness.

泡沫骄傲自满之际

便质疑大海的真实

大笑之后化为空寂

131

Love is an endless mystery,

for it has nothing else to explain it.

爱是无穷奥秘

无物可以释之

132

My clouds, sorrowing in the dark,

forget that they themselves

have hidden the sun.

我的云朵在暗中悲伤

忘记了正是它们自己

把太阳隐藏

133

Man discovers his own wealth

when God comes to ask gifts of him.

当上帝来索取礼物
世人才发现自己的财富

134

You leave your memory as a flame

to my lonely lamp of separation.

你留下你的回忆
宛如火焰
把我离别的孤灯点燃

135

I came to offer thee a flower,

but thou must have all my garden,—

It is thine.

我来给您献一朵花

您却一定要我的整个花园

——您都拿去吧

136

The picture—a memory of light

treasured by the shadow.

图像——

光之记忆

影之珍藏

137

It is easy to make faces at the sun,

He is exposed by his own light in all directions.

对太阳做鬼脸轻而易举

而太阳以自己的光辉

向四面八方展现自己

138

Love remains a secret even when spoken,

for only a lover truly knows that he is loved.

即使说出这个字

也不懂爱的秘密

只有被爱的人

才懂得爱的真谛

139

History slowly smothers its truth,
but hastily struggles to revive it
in the terrible penance of pain.

历史慢慢地扼杀真相
而又在痛苦忏悔中
匆匆地努力矫枉

140

My work is rewarded in daily wages,
I wait for my final value in love.

我的付出已得到每日的报偿
我等待最终的价值以爱计量

141

Beauty knows to say,"Enough."
Barbarism clamours for still more.

美懂得知足常乐
野蛮却贪得无厌

142

God loves to see in me, not his servant,
but himself who serves all.

上帝乐于从我身上看到的
不是他的仆役
而是服务大众的他自己

143

The darkness of night is in harmony with day,
the morning of mist is discordant.

夜之黑暗与白昼和睦共处
雾霭之晨却与之格格不入

144

In the bounteous time of roses love is wine,—
it is food in the famished hour
when their petals are shed.

在玫瑰盛开的充裕时光
爱是佳酿
在落英缤纷的饥馑岁月
爱是食粮

145

An unknown flower in a strange land

speaks to the poet:

"Are we not of the same soil, my lover?"

无名花开,异域芬芳

私语诗人唤情郎

"或恐是同乡?"

146

I am able to love my God

because He gives me freedom to deny Him.

我爱我的上帝

因为上帝给我拒绝他的权利

147

My untuned strings beg for music

in their anguished cry of shame.

我那失调的琴弦

用羞愧的痛苦呻吟

乞求乐音

148

The worm thinks it strange and foolish

that man does not eat his books.

人类不吃自己的书籍

蛀虫认为愚蠢而怪异

149

The clouded sky to-day bears the vision
of the shadow of a divine sadness
on the forehead of brooding eternity.

今天,乌云密布的天空
把神圣忧伤之影的幻象
刻在沉思的永恒之额上

150

The shade of my trees is for passers-by,
its fruit for the one for whom I wait.

我的树给路人以绿荫
而果实只留给心上人

151

Flushed with the glow of sunset
earth seems like a ripe fruit
ready to be harvested by night.

大地被晚霞映红了脸庞
宛如成熟之果
等待夜晚来收获

152

Light accepts darkness for his spouse
for the sake of creation.

为万物之计
光与暗结为伉俪

153

The reed waits for his master's breath,
the Master goes seeking for his reed.

芦笛在等待他主人的气息
天主在四处寻找他的芦笛

154

To the blind pen the hand that writes is unreal
its writing unmeaning.

对于盲目之笔
书写之手并不真实
写作亦无意义

155

The sea smites his own barren breast

because he has no flowers to offer to the moon.

大海捶打他自己贫瘠的胸膛

因为他没有鲜花来献给月亮

156

The greed for fruit misses the flower.

贪婪于果

错失花朵

157

God in His temple of stars
waits for man to bring him his lamp.

在他群星璀璨的神殿
神等待凡人献上灯盏

158

The fire restrained in the tree fashions flowers.
Released from bonds, the shameless flame
dies in barren ashes.

树中节制之火
化为繁花似锦
摆脱束缚的无耻之焰
化为荒芜的灰烬

159

The sky sets no snare to capture the moon,
it is her own freedom which binds her.

天空不曾布下俘获月亮的罗网
是月亮的自由把自己束缚在天上

The light that fills the sky
seeks its limit in a dew-drop on the grass.

布满天空的光
在草上的露珠里寻觅它的边疆

160

Wealth is the burden of bigness,
Welfare the fulness of being.

财富乃伟大之负担
幸福乃存在之圆满

161

The razor-blade is proud of its keenness
when it sneers at the sun.

刀片以锋利自傲
竟把太阳嘲笑

162

The butterfly has leisure to love the lotus,
not the bee busily storing honey.

蝴蝶有闲暇 爱慕莲花
蜜蜂无闲情 贮蜜匆匆

163

Child, thou, bringest to my heart
the babble of the wind and the water,
the flowers' speechless secrets, the clouds' dreams,
the mute gaze of wonder of the morning sky.

孩子呵，你给我的心带来
风与水的潺潺激荡
花朵无言的秘密，云彩的梦想
清晨天空惊奇的默默凝望

164

The rainbow among the clouds may be great
but the little butterfly among the bushes is greater.

云间的彩虹蔚为大观
丛中的小蝶愈加不凡

165

The mist weaves her net round the morning,
captivates him, and makes him blind.

雾霭围绕清晨织网
迷惑他并使他目盲

166

The Morning Star whispers to Dawn,

"Tell me that you are only for me."

"Yes," she answers,

"And also only for that nameless flower."

晨星对黎明低语着

"告诉我，你只是为我"

"是的，"黎明回答说

"也只为那无名的花朵"

167

The sky remains infinitely vacant

for earth there to build its heaven with dreams.

天空保留着无尽空闲的地方

以便大地可以用梦建造天堂

168

Perhaps the crescent moon smiles in doubt
at being told that it is a fragment
awaiting perfection.

当听说自己只是尚待圆满的残片
新月或许会露出将信将疑的笑颜

169

Let the evening forgive the mistakes of the day
and thus win peace for herself.

让黄昏原谅白昼的错误
由此为她自己赢得和睦

170

Beauty smiles in the confinement of the bud,
in the heart of a sweet incompleteness.

在蓓蕾的深闺幽苑
在甜蜜的未臻圆满的花蕊间
美浅笑嫣然

171

Your flitting love lightly brushed with its wings
my sun-flower
and never asked if it was ready to surrender
its honey.

你飘忽不定的爱意
用翅膀轻拂我的向日葵
可从来不曾问起
它是否愿意献出花蜜

172

Leaves are silences

around flowers which are their words.

叶在花的身边

叶沉默

花是叶的语言

173

The tree bears its thousand years

as one large majestic moment.

树木承载千年岁月

恍若宏大一刻

174

My offerings are not for the temple
at the end of the road,
but for the wayside shrines
that surprise me at every bend.

我的奉献
不为道路尽头的宝殿
而为途中每一次峰回路转
给我惊喜的路旁神龛

175

Your smile, my love, like the smell of a strange flower,
is simple and inexplicable.

吾爱，你浅笑嫣然
如同奇花的芬芳
简单而又妙不可言

176

Death laughs when the merit of the dead is exaggerated
for it swells his store with more than he can claim.

当死者的美德被夸张
死神便放声大笑
因为这使他的库存膨胀
超出了他的能量

177

The sigh of the shore follows in vain
the breeze that hastens the ship
across the sea.

海岸的悲鸣
徒劳地追随着
催使船儿飘洋过海的清风

178

Truth loves its limits,

for there it meets the beautiful.

真爱它的极限
那是与美邂逅的地点

179

Between the shores of Me and Thee

there is the loud ocean, my own surging self,

which I long to cross.

在我和你的两岸之间
有喧嚣的海洋相隔
那便是我渴望横渡的
波涛汹涌的自我

180

The right to possess boasts foolishly
of its right to enjoy.

占有的权利
愚蠢地夸示
它享受的权利

181

The rose is a great deal more
than a blushing apology for the thorn.

玫瑰远远不止是为她的刺
而表达的羞涩的歉意

182

Day offers to the silence of stars

his golden lute to be tuned

for the endless life.

白昼请沉默的繁星
给他的金色之琴调音
为他无尽的生命奏鸣

183

The wise know how to teach,

the fool how to smite.

智者懂得如何教化
愚者知道怎样惩罚

184

The centre is still and silent in the heart
of an eternal dance of circles.

圆舞旋转不停
圆心静止无声

185

The judge thinks that he is just when he compares
the oil of another's lamp
with the light of his own.

拿别人的灯油与自己的灯光相比
法官却认为自己公正无私

186

The captive flower in the King's wreath
smiles bitterly when the meadow-flower
envies her.

国王花环上的花露出苦涩的笑意
而草地上的野花却对她羡慕无比

187

Its store of snow is the hill's own burden,
its outpouring of streams is borne by all the world.

积雪是山自己的负担
而喷涌的溪流
却由整个世界承担

188

Listen to the prayer of the forest

for its freedom in flowers.

且听森林的祈祷之声

为它的自由绽放而鸣

189

Let your love see me

even through the barrier of nearness.

且穿越这咫尺天涯

让你的爱看见我吧

190

The spirit of work in creation is there
to carry and help the spirit of play.

对于游戏之魂的支撑
便是创造之魂的使命

191

To carry the burden of the instrument,
count the cost of its material,
and never to know that it is for music,
is the tragedy of deaf life.

携着乐器的负重
算计着材料费用
却永远不知为音乐而生
这便是悲惨的聋聩人生

192

Faith is the bird that feels the light
and sings when the dawn is still dark.

当黎明依然暗淡无光
信仰便是那飞鸟
它迎接曙光并放声歌唱

193

I bring to thee, night, my day's empty cup
to be cleansed with thy cool darkness
for a new morning's festival.

黑夜呵
我把白昼的空杯给你
用你凉爽的黑暗清洗
以待崭新早晨的节日

194

The mountain fir, in its rustling,
modulates the memory of its fights with the storm
into a hymn of peace.

山上的冷杉飒飒作响
它把抗击风暴的过往
变奏为赞颂和平的诗行

195

God honoured me with his fight
when I was rebellious,
He ignored me when I was languid.

当我桀骜不驯
上帝敬我以斗志
当我慵懒无神
上帝便把我忽视

196

The sectarian thinks
that he has the sea
ladled into his private pond.

思想偏狭者自以为
他已将汪洋
舀进了自家的池塘

197

In the shady depth of life
are the lonely nests of memories
that shrink from words.

记忆的孤巢逃避着言语
隐藏在生命的幽暗深处

198

Let my love find its strength
in the service of day,
its peace in the union of night.

让我的爱
在白昼的效劳中获得力量
在黑夜的和谐中觅得安详

199

Life sends up in blades of grass
its silent hymn of praise
to the unnamed Light.

草叶是生命向未名之光
献上的无声的赞美诗行

200

The stars of night are to me

the memorials of my day's faded flowers.

夜晚的繁星对我而言
是我白昼凋零之花的纪念

201

Open thy door to that which must go,

for the loss becomes unseemly when obstructed.

打开你的门户
要去的且由他去
因为阻拦得不偿失

202

True end is not in the reaching of the limit,
but in a completion which is limitless.

真正的终点
并非抵达极限
而是无限地臻于圆满

203

The shore whispers to the sea:
"Write to me what thy waves struggle to say."
The sea writes in foam again and again
and wipes off the lines in a boisterous despair.

海岸对大海低语
"请写下你的波浪挣扎的话语"
大海用泡沫写了又写
又在喧闹的绝望中逐行擦去

204

Let the touch of thy finger thrill my life's strings

and make the music thine and mine.

让你的手指抚动我生命的琴弦

弹奏出你我的和弦

205

The inner world rounded in my life like a fruit,

matured in joy and sorrow,

will drop into the darkness of the original soil for

some further course of creation.

内心世界如同果实

在我生命里蜷伏

在喜与悲中成熟

为进一步的造物

行将落叶归根在

故土的幽暗之处

206

Form is in Matter, rhythm in Force,
meaning in the Person.

形由物示
韵由力治
意由人释

207

There are seekers of wisdom and seekers of wealth,
I seek thy company so that I may sing.

世上有智慧的追寻者
也有追逐财富的过客
我独寻求你的相伴
这样我便可以放歌

208

As the tree its leaves, I shed my words on the earth,
let my thoughts unuttered flower in thy silence.

如同树木落叶一样
我的言语洒在大地上
且让我未曾表达的思想
在你的沉默中绽放

209

My faith in truth, my vision of the perfect,
help thee, Master, in thy creation.

主呵
我对真理的信仰
我对完美的想象
来助力你的开创

210

All the delights that I have left

in life's fruits and flowers

let me offer to thee at the end of the feast,

in a perfect union of love.

在盛宴结束之时

且让我把留在生命之花果中的所有欢喜

以水乳交融之爱奉献给你

211

Some have thought deeply and explored the
meaning of thy truth
and they are great;
I have listened to catch the music of thy play
and I am glad.

有人深思并探寻你真理的内涵
他们不凡
我凝神倾听欣赏你演奏的旋律
我心欢喜

212

The tree is a winged spirit
released from the bondage of seed,
pursuing its adventure of life
across the unknown.

挣脱了种子的束缚
树便是插翅的精灵
穿越那未知的事物
追寻探险的生命旅程

213

The lotus offers its beauty to the heaven,
the grass its service to the earth.

莲花献美于天宇
小草服务于大地

214

The sun's kiss mellows into abandonment
the miserliness of the green fruit clinging
to its stem.

太阳之吻
使执着的青涩之果
瓜熟蒂落

215

The flame met the earthen lamp in me,
and what a great marvel of light!

火焰邂逅我内心的陶灯
迸发出多么神奇的光明

216

Mistakes live in the neighbourhood of truth
and therefore delude us.

谬误与真理比邻
因此迷惑了我们

217

The cloud laughed at the rainbow
saying that it was an upstart
gaudy in its emptiness.
The rainbow calmly answered
"I am as inevitably real as the sun himself."

云朵嘲笑虹霓
说它是个暴发户，空虚艳丽
虹霓平静地回应
"我如太阳一样自然真实"

218

Let me not grope in vain in the dark
but keep my mind still in the faith
that the day will break
and truth will appear
in its simplicity.

莫让我在黑暗中徒劳摸索
且让我初心不改,始终信仰
长夜终将迎来曙光
真理将露出纯真的脸庞

219

Through the silent night

I hear the returning vagrant hopes of the morning

knock at my heart.

寂静长夜难寐

我听到清晨的希望浪子回归

正叩响我的心扉

220

My new love comes

bringing to me the eternal wealth of the old.

我的新欢到来

为我携来旧爱的永恒之财

221

The earth gazes at the moon and wonders
that she should have all her music in her smile.

大地凝视着明月暗自惊奇
她的笑语嫣然间充满旋律

222

Day with its glare of curiosity
puts the stars to flight.

好奇的白昼虎视眈眈
受惊的繁星飞去翩翩

223

My mind has its true union with thee, O sky,
at the window which is mine own,
and not in the open
where thou hast thy sole kingdom.

天空呵
我的心与你真正结合
在我自己的窗口
而不在旷野
那里是你独享的王国

224

Man claims God's flowers as his own
when he weaves them in a garland.

凡人用神的花朵编织花冠
竟觊觎把神的花朵霸占

225

The buried city, laid bare to the sun of a new age,
is ashamed that it has lost all its songs.

湮废的城池
在新时代里重见天日
为其遗曲尽失而羞愧不已

226

Like my heart's pain that has long missed its meaning,

the sun's rays robed in dark

hide themselves under the ground.

Like my heart's pain at love's sudden touch,

they change their veil at the spring's call

and come out in the carnival of colours,

in flowers and leaves.

如同我早已失去意义的心痛

身着黑袍的阳光在地下躲藏

如同我突然被爱触碰的心悸

阳光披上花叶的霓裳

在春天的呼唤下改换面纱

在色彩的狂欢中绽放

227

My life's empty flute
waits for its final music
like the primal darkness
before the stars came out.

我生命空寂的长笛
等待着最后的旋律
正如繁星出现之前
那最初的黑暗幽谧

228

Emancipation from the bondage of the soil
is no freedom for the tree.

从泥土的束缚中获得解救
对树木来说并非自由

229

The tapestry of life's story is woven
with the threads of life's ties
ever joining and breaking.

人生因缘之线
断续相连
织成人生故事的花毯

230

Those thoughts of mine that are never captured by words
perch upon my songs and dances.

我那未被文字俘获的思想
便栖息于我的歌与舞之上

231

My soul to-night loses itself

in the silent heart of a tree

standing alone among the whispers of immensity.

今夜

在一株树沉默的心里

我的心灵迷失了自己

在无尽的低语中茕茕孑立

232

Pearl shells cast up by the sea

on death's barren beach,—

a magnificent wastefulness of creative life.

大海把珍珠的贝壳

抛向死亡的荒滩

这是创造生命的大肆挥霍

233

The sunlight opens for me the world's gate,
love's light its treasure.

阳光为我开启这世界之门
爱之光让我领略稀世之珍

234

My life like the reed with its stops,
has its play of colours
through the gaps in its hopes and gains.

我的人生如同多节的芦管
在希望与收获的孔隙间
吹奏出多彩的和弦

235

Let not my thanks to thee
rob my silence of its fuller homage.

别让我对你的感激
剥夺我的沉默里
对你满满的敬意

236

Life's aspirations come
in the guise of children.

人生的志向
以孩童的装扮登场

237

The faded flower sighs

that the spring has vanished for ever.

落花把春叹

一去不回还

238

In my life's garden

my wealth has been of the shadows and lights

that are never gathered and stored.

在我人生的园中

财富如影似光

不曾被收集和储藏

239

The fruit that I have gained for ever

is that which thou hast accepted.

你已接纳的那只果

便是我永远之所获

240

The jasmine knows the sun to be her brother

in the heaven.

茉莉花知道太阳

是她天上的兄长

241

Light is young, the ancient light;
shadows are of the moment, they are born old.

古老之光,依然年轻
瞬间之影,未秋先零

242

I feel that the ferry of my songs at the day's end
will bring me across to the other shore
from where I shall see.

我感觉我歌声的渡船
在白昼的终点
将载我去往彼岸
在那里我将慧眼明辨

243

The butterfly flitting from flower to flower
ever remains mine,
I lose the one that is netted by me.

流连花间的蝴蝶
永远归属于我
被我网住的那只
我却失去了它

244

Your voice, free bird, reaches my sleeping nest,

and my drowsy wings dream

of a voyage to the light

above the clouds.

自由之鸟

你的声音飞进我沉睡之巢

而我困倦的翅膀

梦见向云上之光的翱翔

245

I miss the meaning of my own part

in the play of life

because I know not of the parts

that others play.

人生如戏

我不懂我的角色的意义

因为对于别人的角色

我一无所知

246

The flower sheds all its petals

and finds the fruit.

繁花落尽始见果

247

I leave my songs behind me
to the bloom of the ever-returning honeysuckles
and the joy of the wind from the south.

我在身后留下我的歌声
留给岁岁绽放的忍冬
留给南方吹来的欢乐的风

248

Dead leaves when they lose themselves in soil
take part in the life of the forest.

枯叶香消玉殒于大地
便与森林融为了一体

249

The mind ever seeks its words

from its sounds and silence

as the sky from its darkness and light.

心灵在其声响和沉默间不断寻觅文字

正如天空在其黑暗与光明间寻觅言辞

250

The unseen dark plays on his flute

and the rhythm of light

eddies into stars and suns,

into thoughts and dreams.

无形的黑暗吹奏着长笛

光明的韵律

围绕着繁星与太阳

涌入了思绪和梦里

251

My songs are to sing

that I have loved Thy singing.

我的歌声唱响

我已爱上您的歌唱

252

When the voice of the Silent touches my words

I know him therefore I know myself.

当沉默之声触摸我的文字

我懂了他,由此也懂了自己

253

My last salutations are to them

who knew me imperfect and loved me.

我把最后的致敬献给他们

那些知道我不完美仍爱我的人

254

Love's gift cannot be given,

it waits to be accepted.

爱的礼物无法恩赐

它等着爱人的同意

255

When death comes and whispers to me

"Thy days are ended,"

let me say to him,"I have lived in love

and not in mere time."

He will ask "Will thy songs remain?"

I shall say "I know not, but this I know

that often when I sang I found my eternity."

当死神走近,细语低沉:

"你的时日已尽。"

且让我对他说:

"我活在爱中,不曾虚度光阴。"

他会问:"你的歌能否长存?"

我会说:"我不知道,

但我知道常常在我欢唱的时辰,

我发现永恒的来临。"

256

"Let me light my lamp,"

says the star,

"And never debate

if it will help to remove the darkness."

星星说:

　"且让我点亮我的灯盏,

而不去争辩,

它是否会消减黑暗。"

257

Before the end of my journey

may I reach within myself

the one which is the all,

leaving the outer shell

to float away with the drifting multitude

upon the current of chance and change.

在我的旅程结束之前

愿我抵达包容一切的内心

且抛下外在的躯身

在偶然与变化的洪流上

与漂泊的众生一同流浪

译后记

泰戈尔生前共计出版过九部英文诗集，其中包括《飞鸟集》《新月集》《园丁集》《吉檀迦利》等，这些诗集从二十世纪二十年代开始由郑振铎和冰心等人陆续译介到中国，一直受到广大中国读者的喜爱。

而《流萤集》是这些诗集中最晚问世的一部，于1928年由麦克米伦公司出版发行，至今已经九十年了。《流萤集》源于泰戈尔的中国和日本之行，在形式和表现手法上受到了日本俳句和中国绝句的影响，短小简洁而又意味深长，与《飞鸟集》堪称泰戈尔的短诗双璧。

如果说《飞鸟集》是这些诗集中对中国影响最大的一部，那么《流萤集》便是与中国渊源最深的一部。《流萤集》中的题赠之诗，其间不乏泰戈尔中国之行中的逸闻逸事。1924年泰戈尔访华期间，徐志摩与林徽因曾追随其左右，参与翻译与接待工作，泰戈尔耳闻目睹了徐对林的爱恋，也认为他俩是理想的一对，便有意促成徐林二人的好事，无奈林已芳心有所属。泰戈尔在给林徽因的赠诗"天之蓝渴望地之绿，徒留其间风的叹息"（《流萤集》之66）中表达了他未能当成月老的遗憾与惆怅。

《飞鸟集》译介到中国已近百年，出现了众多的中文译本，在中国读者中早已深入人心、家喻户晓。而与之难分伯仲的《流萤集》却鲜为人知，直到二十世纪七八十年代才被译成中文。

自去年4月我重译的《飞鸟集》面世以来，不少朋友在给我支持与鼓励之余，也表达了我能重译泰戈尔的其他诗集的期望。出于个人对短诗的偏好，我最终选择了《流萤集》作为我的第二部译诗集。

我有幸在国家图书馆看到了1928年麦克米伦公司出版的英文原版《FIREFLIES》，但令人遗憾的是其中有六页的内容缺失。后来我请在美国工作的同学辗转从弗吉尼亚大学图书馆找到了同一版本的英文原版书，补上了缺失的六页内容，并以此作为我翻译的底本。

又一个岁末年初，几十个寒夜的灯下，我再次徜徉于诗情画意与哲理的诗丛，与诗人进行跨越时空的心与心的交流。偶尔眺望窗外的夜空，我仿佛看见微弱闪烁的流萤之光，在引领我寻觅光明的方向。

最后，我愿以《流萤集》中的这句诗与读者朋友们共勉：

> 天空没有留下翅膀的痕迹
> 但我为曾经的飞翔而欣喜

王钦刚

2018年3月